101 Lessons
from
Enterprise Architecture

Roger Evernden

ISBN: 1502835657
ISBN-13: 978-1502835659

DEDICATION

For the three people in my life that make everything
worthwhile: Elaine, Keith and Christopher

Contents

ACKNOWLEDGMENTS

I am indebted to the many enterprise architects that I've known and worked with. The ideas in this book are drawn from the initiatives and projects that I've been involved with. I feel fortunate that I've had the opportunity to learn from these colleagues and friends over the years.

I also owe a debt to Matthew Frederick, who wrote 101 Things I Learned in Architecture School – a fascinating book, and the inspiration for me to search for 101 Lessons from Enterprise Architecture!

I am also deeply indebted to my best friend and partner – Elaine. As always, she is my support, my encouragement and my inspiration.

INTRODUCTION

Several years ago I came across a book by Matthew Frederick – "101 Things I Learned in Architecture School". I started thinking about things that I had learned from Enterprise Architecture, and that's how this book started. It doesn't cover everything that I've learned from enterprise architecture, but it does cover some of the things that matter, a few that get overlooked, and some that were a challenge to write explain in a couple of paragraphs and a diagram.

Because much of what I've learned applies to design as much as to architecture, I've sometimes referred to "design", sometimes "architecture", and sometimes both. I've kept the lessons as general as possible, so that they apply to as many situations and contexts as possible.

One thing I've found is that the lessons from enterprise architecture are different from the lessons of building architecture. This book is my attempt to write down some of those lessons and ideas.

101 Lessons from Enterprise Architecture is a bit tongue-in-cheek, and it's certainly a departure from some of my other writings about the subject, but I hope you enjoy reading it as much as I enjoyed writing it!

1. WAYS OF WORKING (WOW)

Many methodologies are described by their chief characteristic.

The steps in a "waterfall methodology" resemble a cascading waterfall. A "rapid development method" produces fast results. A methodology might be "object oriented".

But this is only ever a promise. A methodology can only ever be a guideline, a methodical way of working.

Remember that the pressures of day-to-day work bring workarounds and exceptions that compromise any theory.

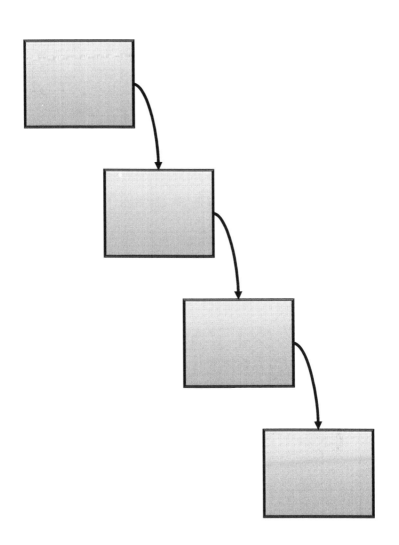

2. VALUE DEPENDS MORE ON DYNAMIC ELEMENTS THAN STATIC ONES

The components and structure of an architecture or design are important as a foundation. But without relationships and interfaces between the parts they lack energy.

A design is useful and worthwhile because it does something - it has a purpose. The static elements alone are like a mortgage: no-one wants a mortgage; they want what the mortgage offers, the possibility of buying a home.

Static elements provide a basis. The connections make it interesting – they provide dynamics, interaction, energy, and potential.

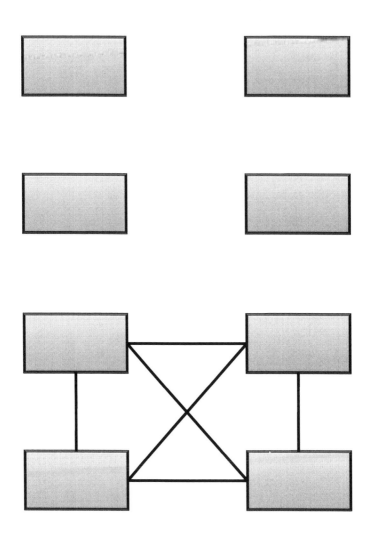

3. EACH EXPERIENCE IS STRONGLY INFLUENCED BY HOW WE ARRIVE AT IT

Pathways, interfaces and connections are vital. A vast cathedral interior appears greater when we enter through a much smaller doorway.

We may find information through a search engine, through the interface of an application, or by following a process. Their usability affects our experience.

The journey to a program or component in an architecture or design affects what we feel about it and how we use it.

Make each journey memorable and interesting.

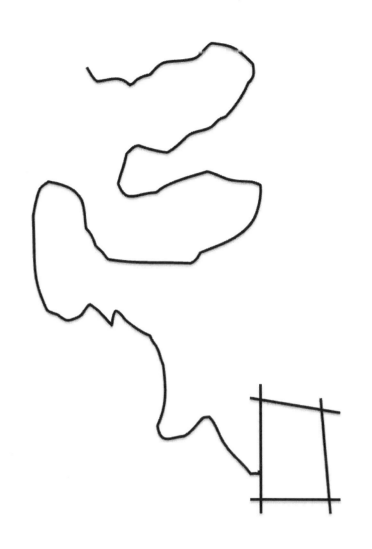

4. EACH COMPONENT IS INFLUENCED BY SURROUNDING COMPONENTS

Software users generally use more than one program at a time. Someone might use a calendar and address book, an Internet search engine, and a photo editor to plan a Golden Wedding party.

How these applications work together determines whether this is easy or difficult, enabling or frustrating.

Some components are outside our control. If there is a weak link, it will affect everything else.

Allow for the weaknesses in surrounding components.

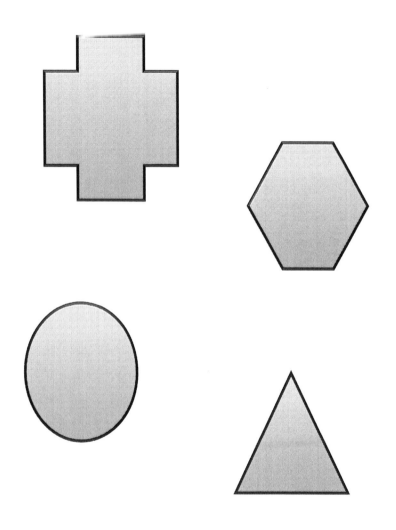

5. SLOW, INACCURATE AND BRILLIANT

It was Einstein who first said that "Computers are incredibly fast, accurate and stupid. Human beings are incredibly slow, inaccurate and brilliant. Together they are powerful beyond imagination."

Architectures and designs should work well with people.

They should allow time for people to interact, to reflect, to think, and to imagine.

Allow for people making mistakes, misunderstanding, losing concentration, and being brilliant.

6. MAKE STEADY AND SURE PROGRESS

Activities nearly always take longer than we expect.

Work out how long you think it will take, and then add another 20 to 50%. And even then, half the time you will need to add another 20 to 50%.

The important thing is that we do make sure and steady progress – one step at a time – until the task is complete.

Take the time to measure progress towards your target.

If you're not making progress, make the changes necessary to ensure progress towards a goal or objective.

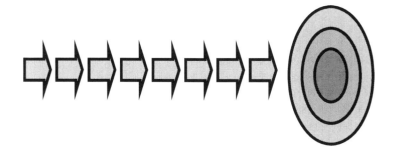

7. OPEN-ENDED DESIGN

The best designs are those that allow people to use them in ways beyond those thought up by the designer. The design can handle each user's creative adaptations.

Create architectures and designs that aren't too restrictive. Design pieces that can be combined in many ways. Only impose limits for safety or compliance.

Make it easy to change business or process rules to cater for new situations, or to support needs that weren't thought of at the time of the initial requirements.

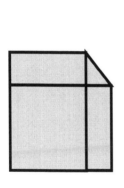
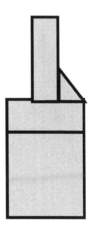

8. THE VALUE IN BITS AND BYTES

The design of musical notation gives a composer or musician a wonderfully flexible and creative tool.

Nuts and bolts, plugs and sockets, bricks and mortar are all design elements – created out of the context in which they are finally used. They are designed without the final end in mind.

When you've created a big design, look at it again to see if there are smaller elements that could be used and used and reused.

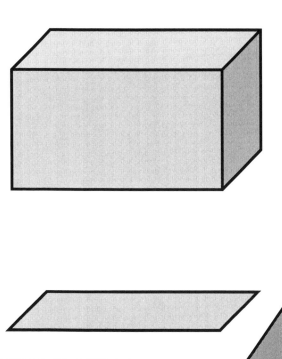

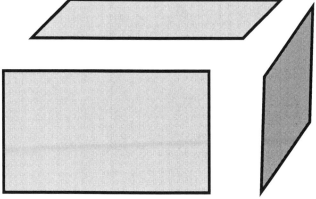

9. DISCARDED PIECES MAY HAVE THE GERM OF THE NEXT IDEA

Pieces that don't fit into one architecture or design are often valuable later.

Much can be harvested from what we frequently waste.

Keep a scrapbook of things that might have been discarded, and review it periodically.

It will often inspire or suggest new ideas. Sometimes you will have something that you can simply reuse.

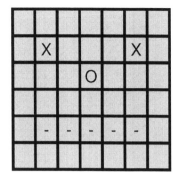
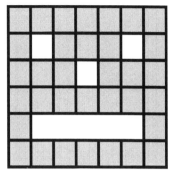

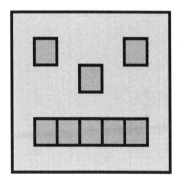

10. THE NATURE OF LOGIC

There is logic to the structure of a design, and there is logic to how a design is used. The two are very different in nature.

The logic of structure explains how elements are combined to form a complete design.

The logic of use explains the flow of using the elements in the context of the complete design.

Separate the logic of structure from the logic of use to make a design more flexible and adaptable.

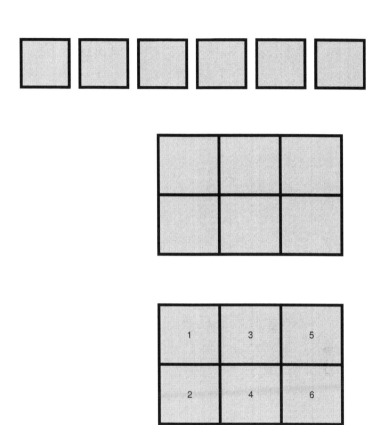

11.   SEPARATE THE DYNAMIC FROM THE STATIC

Things change. But some things change more frequently and more rapidly than others.

Discover which bits of the design are likely to change most often. Then find ways to make it easy for these pieces to change.

Make elements that are less likely to change more stable and fixed. These are the anchors that make it easy to change the dynamic elements.

| 1 | 2 | A | 3 | 4 | B |

| 1 | 2 | C | 3 | 4 | F |

| 1 | 2 | E | 3 | 4 | C |

| 1 | 2 | E | 3 | 4 | D |

12. OLD SOLUTIONS AND NEW SOLUTIONS

Old problems have a history of old design solutions. Some are good, some bad. But we can learn from old solutions – taking them as a starting point and building on experience - for our new designs.

New problems don't have the same history. Instead we must focus on ingenuity, originality, and fresh thinking. New skills, knowledge, familiarity and know-how must be developed.

With old problems, avoid getting stuck in a rut by repeating old designs.

Use new problems to stimulate design, and even inspire new solutions to old problems.

13. ARRANGEMENT VERSUS COMPLEXITY

Arrangement turns complicated problems into simpler ones.

Arrangement helps break a big problem into smaller sections.

Look for patterns. Rearrange elements until they make more sense.

There is often an arrangement that is less complex and easier to understand.

Play with elements one piece at a time; gradually structure will emerge.

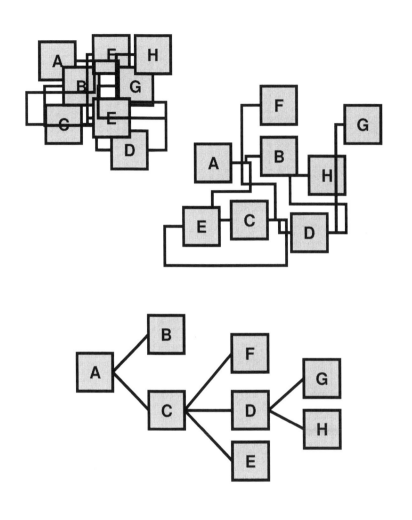

14. CURRENT USE AND FUTURE POSSIBILITIES

Studying how people use a design today is not necessarily a good way to anticipate how they might use it in the future. An apparently small innovation or change can completely change how people use an existing design.

Hypertext links can totally change a previously sequential flow.

Absence of a better tool frequently leads to new uses for an old tool.

Although the initial design can't anticipate all future possibilities, create a design that can anticipate probable changes

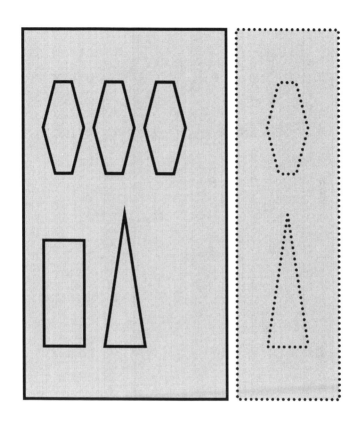

15. CERTAINTY IS A RARITY

We rarely know exactly how people are going to use designs or architectures.

Although we seek certainty, ambiguity is the norm.

Certainty may simplify, but it can also lead to predictable, dull and boring.

Embrace uncertainty. It could be said that uncertainty, ambiguity, imprecise requirements and unclear goals are the type of things that drive creativity, innovation, and originality in our solutions.

$$2 + 2 \boxed{= 4}$$

$$>6 + <3 \boxed{= ?}$$

16. SYSTEMATIC DESIGN

Systematic design would require a complete understanding of what is required and why it is needed.

Uncertainty, difficulty in finding or expressing requirements, confusion, misunderstanding, opinions, bias, and a whole host of other factors make complete understanding impossible.

Time and resource constraints impose further limitations.

Be aware that systematic is a relative, rather than an absolute term. It is an aspiration rather than a realization.

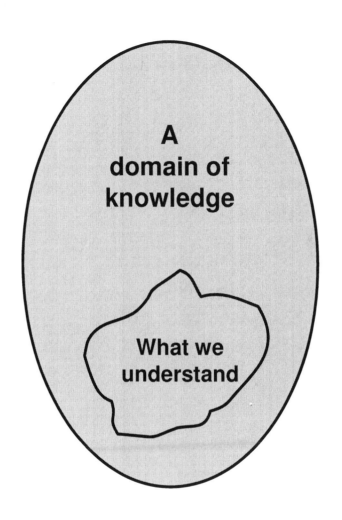

17. GOOD DETECTIVES AND BAD CRIMINALS

In an article called "Keeping It Simple", John Seely Brown and Paul Duguid compare the relationship between users and designers to a relationship between good detectives and bad criminals.

Good detectives – the users – consciously look for and unconsciously pick up clues on how to use the design.

As a designer or an architect, be like the bad criminal – leave plenty of clues for the users to find.

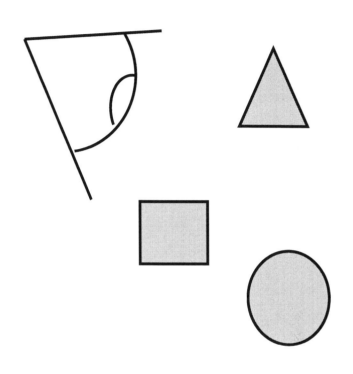

18.   UNPREDICTABILITY

Increasingly people will use architectures or designs in places we can't predict. Word processing software, originally designed for use by someone using a desktop computer, might be used on a laptop, or phone, or television.

Or on a crowded train; deep in the Brazilian rainforest; orbiting earth in a space station.

For example: to document a team discussion or distribute homework to a class of 30 children.

Design for use in unpredictable situations or locations.

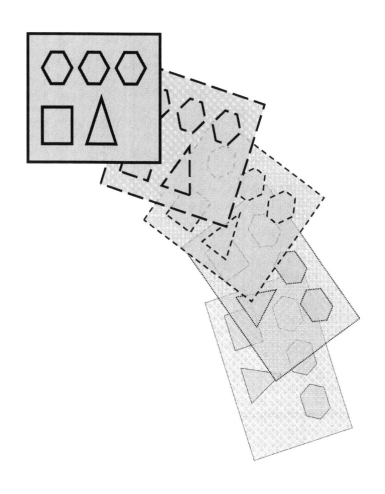

19. NOBODY EXPECTS THE UNEXPECTED - BEYOND THE EXPECTED - GREAT UNEXPECTATIONS

For a given type of architecture or design, there is a basic or expected functionality. For example, all spoons have certain characteristics in common.

The basic or expected functionality is a must – it needs to be included in the design for the design to belong to that type of design. It's difficult to eat soup with a fork.

But good design goes beyond the bare, the mundane and the expected.

Add the unexpected. Create another dimension of things to discover, to elate, to excite and to inspire.

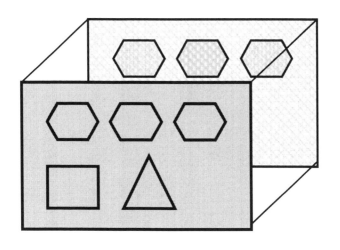

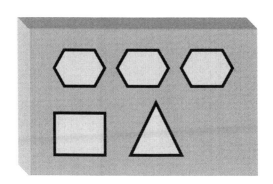

20.   TAKE A STEP OUTSIDE

There comes a time in any analysis or design process when you need to take a break. Have a change of scene.

If you're inside – go outside.

If you're outside - step inside.

Get away from ideas and concepts and thoughts to see what's shaking in the real world [in the words of a John Butler Trio song].

Or escape from reality to the world of ideas and fantasy.

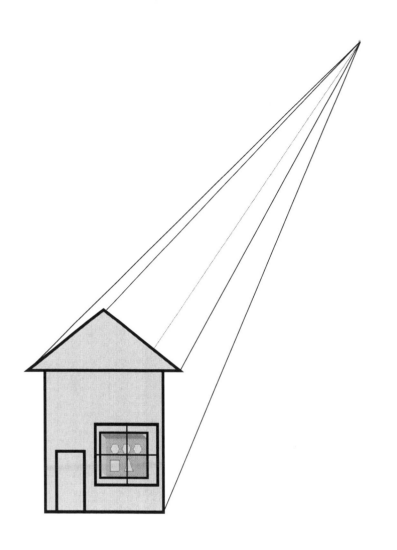

21.   GENERALITY AND SPECIFICITY

It's often easier to design with specific needs in mind and an awareness of any potential for generality, than to design for generality and assume that it will work for all specific needs.

Context guides design. A specific context provides further context.

But if you design for specific needs, remember to test for generality.

And if you design for generality, remember to test for all the specific situations you can think of.

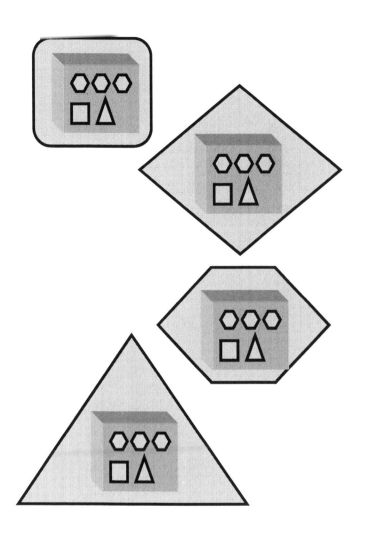

22.　OH WHAT A FEELING

A functional design can fulfill the requirements. It does what was asked.

But a good design needs more than that. Excitement, richness, fun are difficult to explain as requirements. They give feeling to a functional design.

Without feeling a functional design can seem flat, dull and uninteresting.

Inject your designs with enthusiasm, spirit, passion, energy, magnificence, and pleasure.

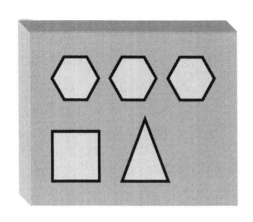

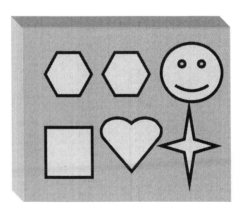

23.   BEWARE THE WOMBAT

I've got nothing against the burrowing antipodean animal, but as an acronym a wombat is a waste of money, brains and time.

Good design needs a sense of purpose and challenges the brain cells. It feels worthwhile and useful. Wasting money, brains and time is demoralizing.

Every now and then, inevitably, a wombat appears. It may not always be apparent at first, but as soon as it is clear that you have a wombat, walk away.

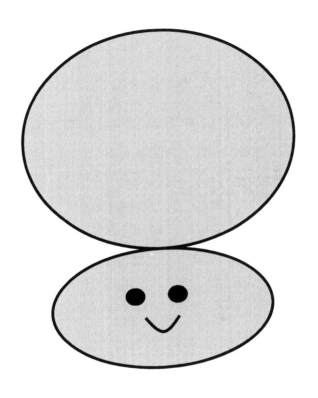

24. TACTICALLY STRATEGIC

Think for the long-term, but act in the short-term.

Be aware of the way that things will probably pan out in the distant future, and create designs that can adapt to those possibilities and probabilities.

But create a design that meets current needs and fulfils an immediate purpose.

This is the design equivalent of Think Globally, Act Locally.

Think Strategically, Act Tactically.

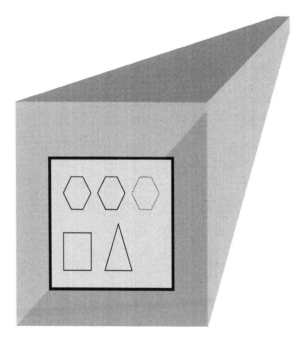

25.   LOOK UP, LOOK DOWN

Sometimes it's easier to look down than to look up – to get immersed in details. And sometimes it's easier to look up – and become too abstract or conceptual.

It's important to do both – to look at a design from a high-level and from a detailed level.

And then to look at it from every other angle – left, right, inside out, outside in.

And view it from the perspective of different people in different roles in different locations from different cultural backgrounds…

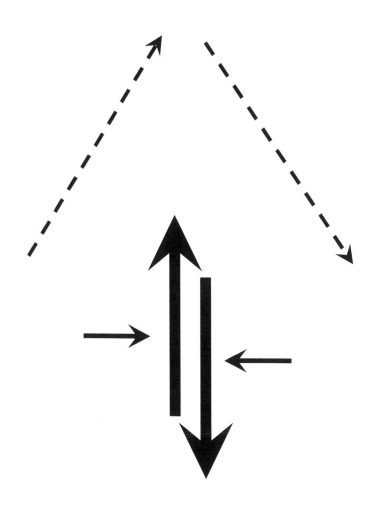

26.   WAYS OF THINKING

A methodology is one way of doing something. It is not the only way.

There may be other methodologies. There may be variations within a methodology. Or there can be ways of doing things that are not documented in a methodology.

Methodologies provide a fall-back structure or a source of ideas rather than a recipe to stick to. As Gerald Weinberg put it - a methodology is a way of thinking – not a substitute for it.

Cherry pick methodology ideas and adapt them to suit your needs.

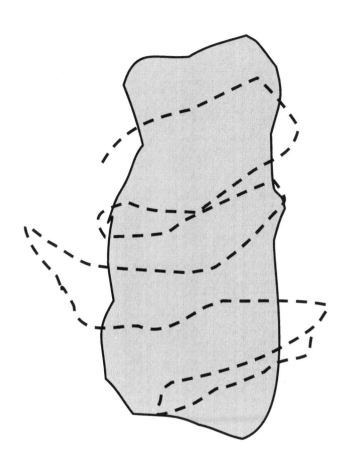

27.   SOLUTIONS AND PROBLEMS

Lawrence J. Peters wrote that every solution creates problems of its own [1981].

Some solutions create more than one new problem.

But then problems lead to solutions!

And more solutions lead to more problems.

Try to be aware of any problems that you are creating through your solutions. And use these problems to generate further solutions.

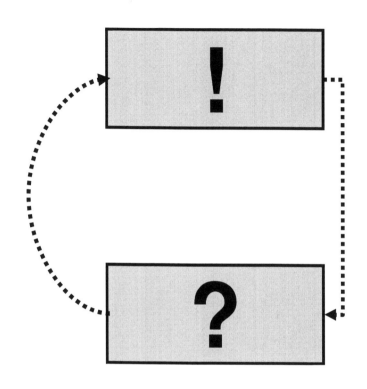

28.   COMPLETENESS

Specifications are never complete. Something could always be added.

It is impossible to get a definitive statement for every detailed requirement.

The specification only needs to be sufficiently complete – complete enough to design a solution; as complete as it needs to be for the purpose at hand.

Don't over-specify. Beyond a point, the effort to be complete exceeds its value – following the law of diminishing returns.

29. THERE IS NO SINGLE SOLUTION

The "correct" solution is always open to interpretation. It is always possible to think of alternatives.

And it is always possible that there is a better solution; or a worse solution.

And there's always room for improvement. That's how things evolve.

Look beyond your first ideas. Consider substitute or complementary ideas. Allow others to make suggestions and improvements

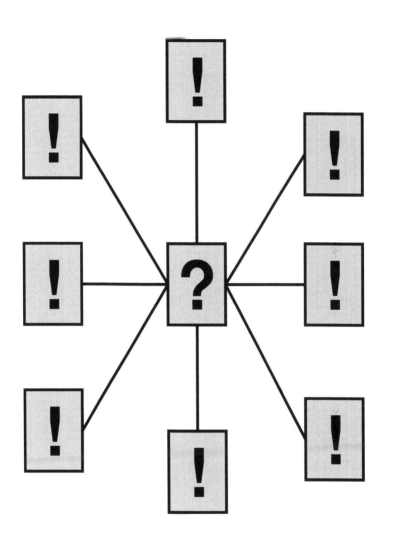

30.   RIGHT OR WRONG

Designs and solutions are appropriate, or unsuitable, fit for purpose, relevant, better or worse, good or bad, within budget or not, delivered on time or late – but not right and not wrong.

Wrong in one context might be right in another.

Define criteria that can be used to evaluate a design to judge how well it meets the need or requirement.

Also use these criteria to assess the relative merits of alternative designs.

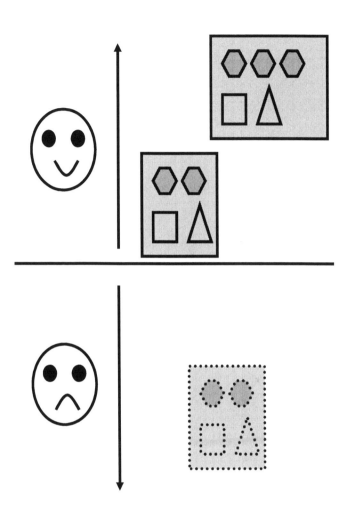

31. ACTIVELY REDUCE ENTROPY

There's a natural tendency for everything to degrade or wear out. We organize files or papers but they will gradually get messy and disorganized again. This is entropy.

We reduce entropy in a filing cabinet by tidying up and reorganizing. The equivalent for ideas and design is introspection or reflection.

Allow time to reflect, tidy up and reorganize. It reduces the possibility of entropy, and feedback from introspection adds value to a design or a system.

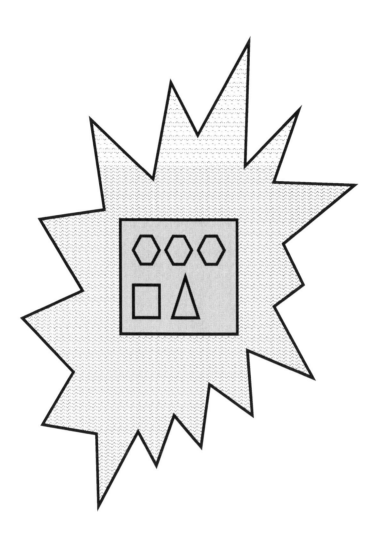

32. SUCCESS IS 80% PERSISTENCE

It won't always work out right first time – in fact, it rarely does!

Figure out what's wrong, what's not working, gather feedback, get another opinion – and try again; and again; and again and again – until it works out.

Learn from mistakes, errors and failures. Then build your success and foundations.

Persistently building and building on your success is the path to delivering strong and powerful designs.

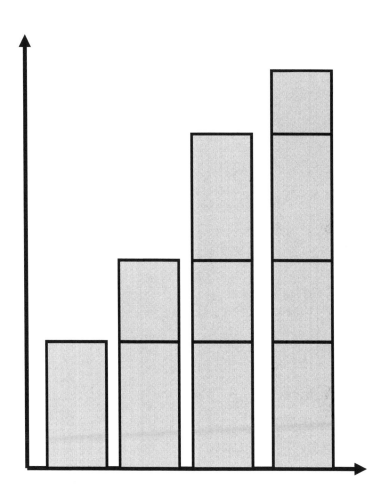

33.   SUCCESS IS 80% PLANNING AND THINKING

OK – that doesn't add up (with the previous 80% claim).

But if you have a plan or design and the commitment to carry it through, then there's a good chance that you'll reach your goal.

It's really a variation on persistence. Time spent planning and thinking will make it easier to act and do.

Dwight D. Eisenhower said: "In preparing for battle I have always found that plans are useless, but planning is indispensable." The planning and the plan both play their part - and you don't get a plan without planning.

100%

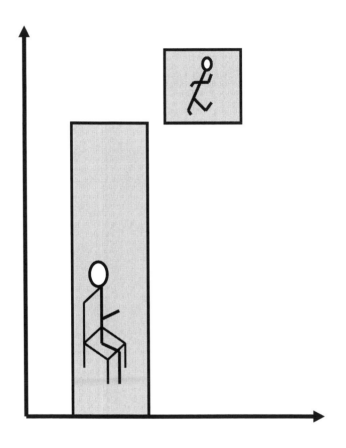

34.   GREEN FOR GO

You wouldn't sit at home waiting for all the traffic lights along a route to go green before you started a journey.

It's impossible to get a green light for everything before you get started. All you need is a green light for the first or next step. Each small, distinct step combines to get you to your destination.

Put 80% of your energy into getting green for the first step.

Then make every step so that you are in a position to make the next step.

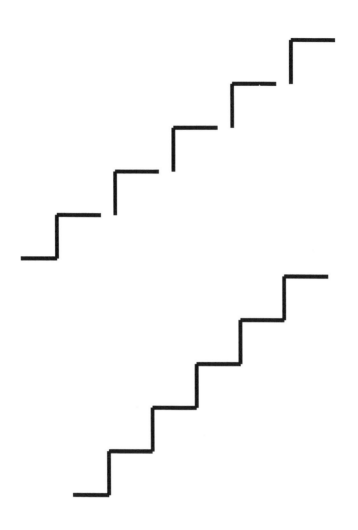

35.   SMALL CHANGE

Should you use two decimal places or three? Even a small change can make a big difference.

But it's not always possible to predict exactly what will be affected by a change. Change A and it impacts B & C; change D and it affects B, E & F.

The impact is often unpredictable until the change is made.

Try to make small changes and make one change at a time. That way it's easier to assess the impact or consequences and know that the change is right.

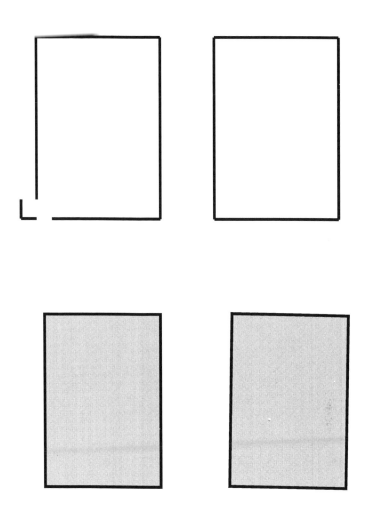

36. ONE FOR ALL AND ALL FOR ONE

Like dominoes or the ripple effect, every aspect of a system (large or small) is affected by many, if not all, of the others.

If it truly is thought of or managed as a system, then the whole is the sum of the parts (and more than the sum of the parts).

Change one part and the overall whole is now different; if the overall thing is different, then the other parts will be affected.

Think holistically. Always keep the big picture in mind when dealing with the parts.

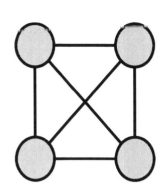

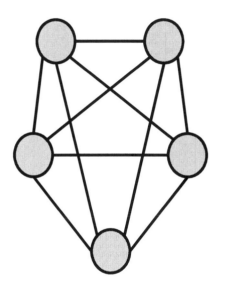

37.   TRIAGE

If everything is connected to everything else, and a change to any part affects all the other parts... it can get very complex and hard to comprehend. As you add more components, then there will be an even greater number of relationships.

One really effective way to deal with this is to group components into meaningful chunks, and then treat the chunk as a component in its own right.

Try chunking in groups of three. This keeps relationships simple, with each component validated by two others.

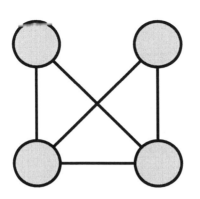

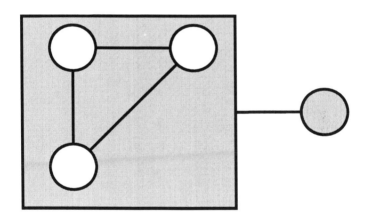

38. NOT ALL SOLUTIONS ARE TECHNOLOGY-BASED

Sometimes the best solution isn't a technology one. (Seriously – it sometimes happens!!)

Don't straitjacket all solutions by technology.

It's sometimes cheaper and better to find an answer that uses brain power or a manual process, rather than jump straight in with a technology solution.

Separate all designs into a human element and a technology element. Only use technology if it really is the best solution.

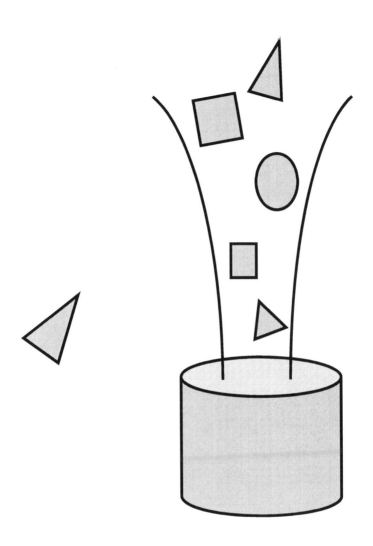

39. DYNAMIC PLANS

It's always a moving target.

Plans and actions need to evolve, dynamically, together. Dynamic projects need dynamic plans.

Long term dynamic projects and developments shouldn't be constrained by static plans.

Revisit plans on a regular basis, and especially when there are significant changes or developments.

Make sure that the plans are as dynamic as the project.

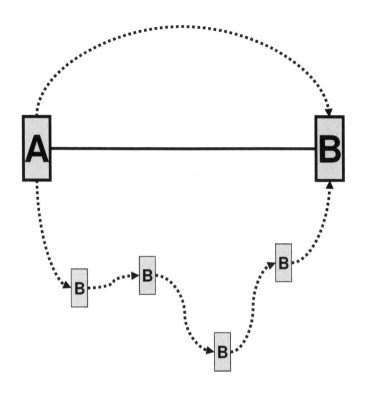

40. PRINCIPLES AND PATTERNS

Principles and patterns can be used in many different situations.

In different ways, each summarizes a set of requirements that would take much more effort to document or record.

Keep plans flexible by guiding developments with principles and patterns, rather than using more complicated requirements.

Only document requirements in a more detailed form when they are cannot be covered by a principle or pattern.

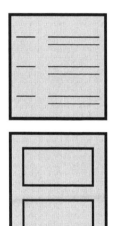

41.   SMART AND DRAMATIC

The most dramatic changes to a design occur through changes to the architecture.

Dramatic changes are fundamental changes – they are changes to the foundations and foundational elements.

Smart changes are often dramatic changes. They often make a big difference. Even when a change is relatively small, if it is a smart change it is also significant.

To identify smart changes, look for key changes in the architecture – in the underpinning groundwork.

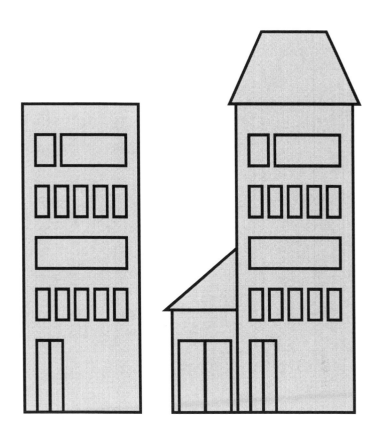

42.   RESOURCE FIT

The basic resources are people, things, money, time and information.

"People" includes skills and experience. "Things" includes equipment, machinery or office space.

The most limited resource will have the biggest impact on your solution or plan.

Design your solutions and manage your plans to fit within the constraints imposed by your most limited resource.

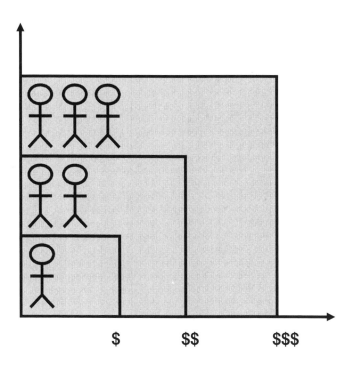

$ $$ $$$

43.   THE EARLY BIRD

Early effort is worth more than catch up effort later.

A centimetre of good planning is worth a metre of design.

A centimetre of good design is worth a metre of implementation.

A centimetre of good implementation is worth a metre of maintenance.

Get it as right as possible at each stage. This will minimize the costly and difficult effort to introduce overlooked elements at a later stage.

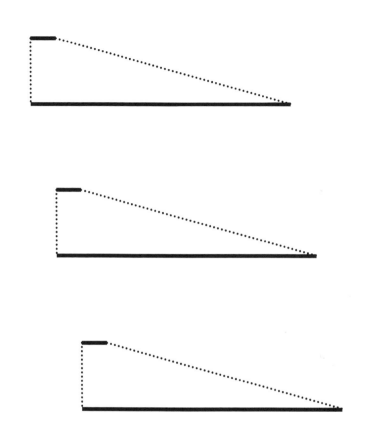

44. VALUE AND IMPORTANCE

You will always be short of time, resources, and skills.

You never know when projects will get canned or resources cut. Delivering value or importance early on increases the chance of survival.

Focus effort on doing the bits that will deliver something of big value or importance as early as possible.

And if you don't get the chance to finish, at least you delivered some value or benefit.

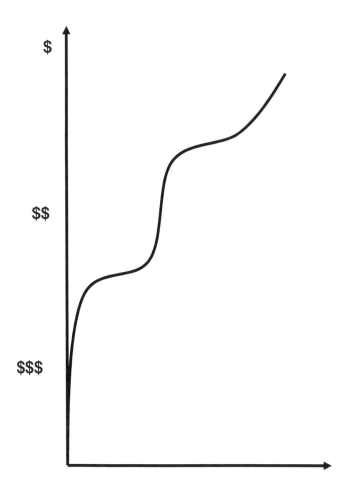

45.   LEARNING ON THE JOB

Any plan or roadmap will be changed as you proceed and learn more about the plan or roadmap.

You gradually get to understand the issues, requirements, politics, governance, funding, dependencies, priorities and all the other details that only become apparent once you've started with a plan or design.

Be prepared to learn as you do. That's what evolutionary design means – the design emerges and is revealed as you go.

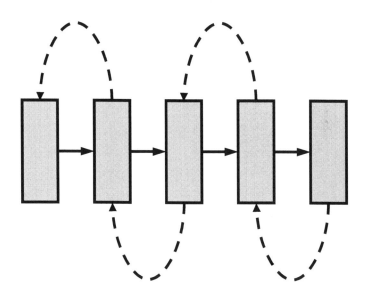

46.   SIMPLE AND ELEGANT

It's easy to think of a difficult and complex solution to a problem.

It's much harder to think of a simple, elegant solution.

More complex solutions are more difficult to implement and maintain.

Simple solutions are easier to implement and maintain.

Keep it simple. Simplify designs wherever possible. Make them easier to understand and quicker to develop. Think about how to minimize any future upkeep.

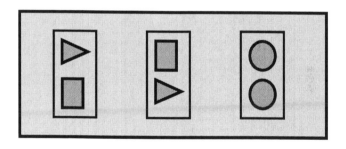

47.   QUESTIONS

e e cummings wrote, "More beautiful the answer from he who asks the more beautiful question."

Ask a simple question and the answer may be simple. Ask a more complicated question and the answer may be more complicated.

The important point is that there are different types of question. Closed questions can be answered with a simple yes / no answer. Open questions require a more detailed response.

Choose the right question to improve chances of getting the right reply.

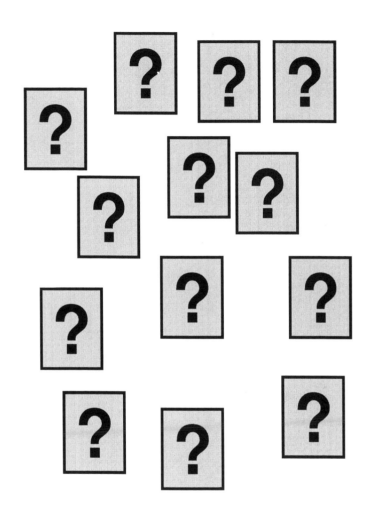

48. DRAWING A BLANK

If you are starting from scratch, try to start from something. It's easier to work with something than nothing. Anything is often better than a void. Avoid blank paper syndrome.

Find something that gets the mind working. It can be something similar or something different – it is only to get you started. Write it down – then refine it. Make a rough estimate then improve it.

The quicker you can get something up and running, the quicker you have something to work with, get feedback, discuss and improve.

49. STEPS OR STAGES

It is easier to grasp a journey, transformation, change, modification, or alteration when it is broken down into simpler steps or stages.

Each step has a smaller result, but is a foundation for the next step.

If the steps are right, the next small and simple step is easier.

If the steps are wrong, then everything else goes awry.

Divide any large or complex program or change into a series of smaller steps or components.

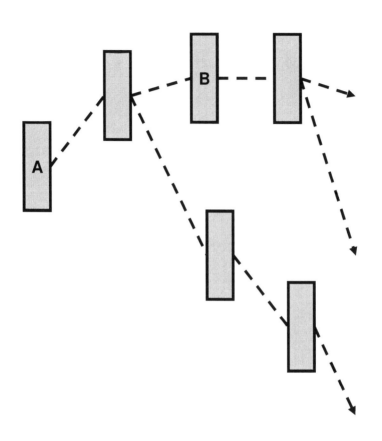

50.   STEP-BY-STEP

The critical step is always the next one. As it has been said many times before - the longest journey begins with the first small step.

Combine this with the first law of wing-walking - don't let go of your hold until you have grasped the next hold.

Choose your steps carefully. And make sure that each step is to solid ground before proceeding.

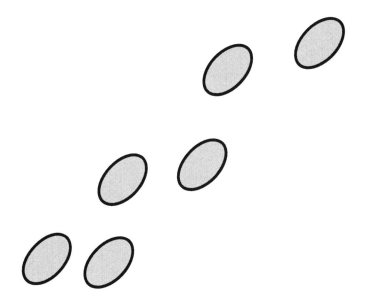

51.   VAGUENESS

Designs and decisions depend on clarity and understanding.

But it is difficult to respond to questions, requirements or statements when they are vague or uncertain. They are open to interpretation, misunderstanding or confusion.

Furthermore, if the requirements are vague, then it is difficult to know whether a proposal or solution is a good response or not.

Similarly, if your designs and solutions are vague then it is difficult to approve or improve them.

Eliminate vagueness. If anything isn't clear, ask more questions.

???

???

???

???

???

???

???

52.   THE FUTURE

It is impossible to know exactly what the future holds.

But you can know about the present, and the past. By gathering information about the present you can get a better idea of what needs to change, why it needs to change, whether it is likely to change, and how it might change.

And we can learn from the past, and use history to identify and predict trends.

Ground the future in information about the present and the past.

53.   KNOW YOU KNOW

Experts know when they don't know. Experts understand when they don't understand.

Non-experts may try to fool you into thinking that they do know or understand.

Questions help to distinguish between experience and expertise, and deception and ignorance.

Ask for sources of information. Ask how someone knows. Get them to explain, and demonstrate that they really know and understand.

54.   PERFECTION

Perfection is impossible and expensive.

The perfect plan, estimate, or design will be expensive, take a long time to produce, and consume a lot of resources.

And it still won't be perfect.

Aim for perfection, but be practical.

Do your best.

And always be aware of, and respond to, feedback, comments or suggestions.

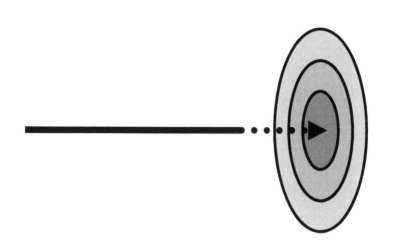

55. THE NEXT LEVEL OF DETAIL

You should always expect to provide the next level of detail.

When you give a high-level overview you will probably get asked about the next level of detail.

And you may be asked about specifics in a more detailed view.

You might need to provide sources for your statements. You might be asked to back up your assertions. And so on.

Always prepare at least one level of detail beyond the one you are planning to show, talk about or demonstrate.

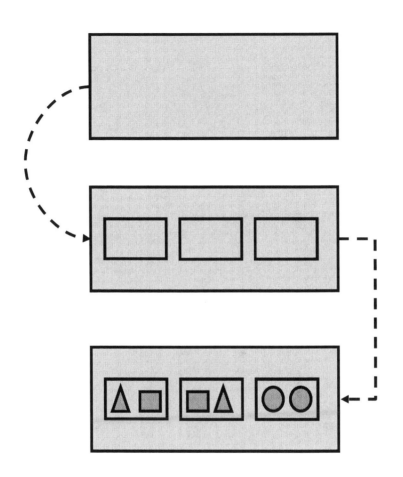

56.   SIMPLIFYING THROUGH ORGANISATION

As you find out more information it is inevitable that requirements, plans and designs grow and become bigger.

It is easier to manage if you can keep things as simple as possible.

Group similar things together.

Use the same format and structure for items that are of a similar type.

Arrange information hierarchically.

Review materials and simplify them.

All of these help to keep things simple.

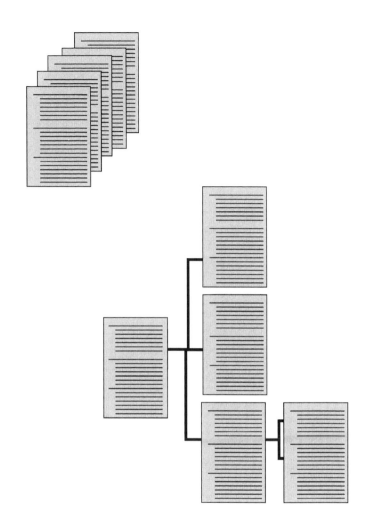

57.   CREATE OR ARRANGE

Is designing or architecting an act of creation - a conscious attempt to break away from the familiar and everyday to create something new and distinctive?

Or is it an awareness of possibilities that are already out there – waiting to be discovered – taking existing elements and arranging them into a pattern or shape?

Mix your personal creative genius with input from the ideas sphere. Fuse the rich source of external ideas with your own distinct interpretation to create an original design.

58.   GOING BACK

Sometimes you have to stop, and even go back rather than go on (I left the key in the door; or left my wallet behind).

Admit mistakes and errors, when they happen.

Go back. Learn. Change targets and plans as necessary.

And then move on.

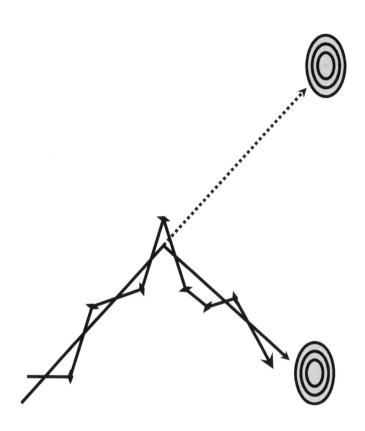

59. DELIVER, DELIVER, DELIVER

Until you deliver something tangible, designs, requirements or concepts remain only as ideas.

Trust begins with tangibles.

People say - I'll believe it when I see it. I'll know the quality is good when I can feel it. I believe your estimates, resource allocation and budgets when I have the final product in my hand.

Look for the deliverables at every stage in the journey. Make them visible. And make sure you actually deliver them – it's what you will be measured on.

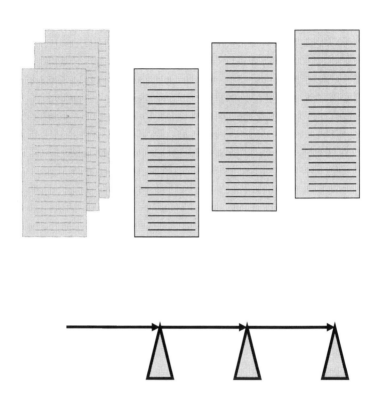

60.   ESTIMATES

Estimates are just that – estimates.

They are simplified, generalized.

They can only ever be based on hypotheses, assumptions and historical data.

Update estimates with more accurate information as soon as possible.

And keep updating them as more facts become available.

61.   VISIBILITY

Always include a parachute.

Always have a contingency plan.

Always consider the risks, constraints, and possible deviations.

These things are often overlooked, or hidden from view, or not made explicit.

Don't overlook or hide them. Consider what you will do if things go wrong and your plans or designs don't work out. Make contingency plans, risks, constraints and alternative outcomes clear to decision makers.

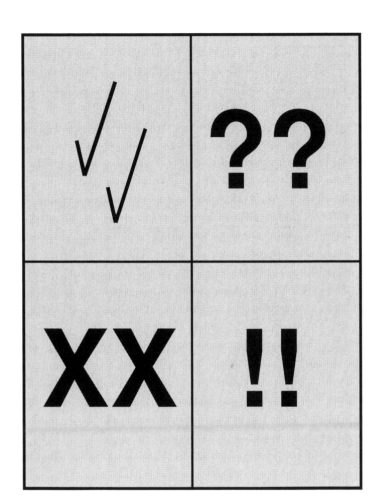

62. TALES OF THE UNEXPECTED

Something nearly always happens that you didn't anticipate.

When something crops up that you didn't foresee, write it down and suggest a solution – a way of dealing with it.

Then bring it to the attention of decision makers, users and customers; and anyone else that might be affected in any way.

Don't delay!

Document and respond positively to the unexpected.

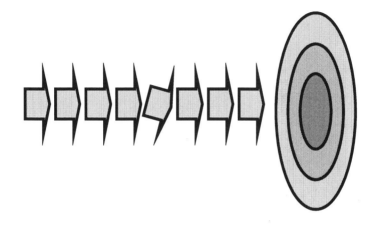

63.   GREAT EXPECTATIONS

What people think you said, think you promised or think you claimed can be - and often is - different from what you actually said, promised or claimed.

If the two don't balance – explain the difference and reset expectations.

Restate what you actually did say, what you are going to do, or what you claimed.

Manage expectations. Because what people expect is what you will need to deliver to maintain credibility and trust.

64.   DECISION LOG

Decisions determine the shape of a design or solution. It is often necessary to explain and justify a decision – sometimes a long time after the decision was made.

Track decisions. Keep a record of key issues and questions and how they were answered.

And record the reason for the decision. This will be quickly lost to posterity if you don't.

And make a note of other considered options that weren't taken – and why they weren't taken.

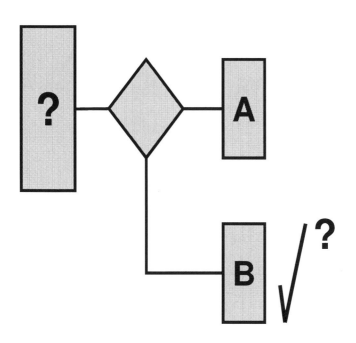

65.   THE SMALL PRINT

When something is written down it has a degree of clarity and permanence that conversations or verbal communications lack.

Make it a habit to put any claims and promises in writing. Don't make any promise without putting it in writing.

State the obvious, because unless it's stated it often isn't obvious!

And writing it down is one way of confirming everything that's been agreed. If it isn't written down, it's open to dispute.

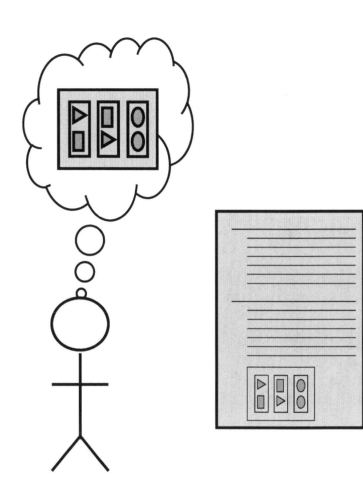

66. CERTAINTY

One thing that's certain is uncertainty.

Changes always happen. You can't anticipate everything.

Don't fight it.

Put in place mechanisms to handle it effectively.

Keep track of requests for changes, to justify and explain why changes are needed, to compare options, and to evaluate the impact of any changes.

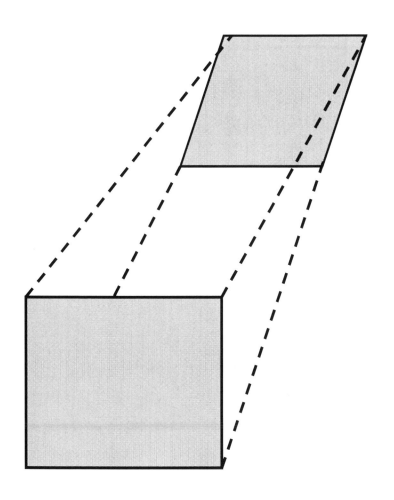

67. TRACEABILITY

Everything depends on everything. There are causal links, dependencies and relationships throughout the design and development process.

Requirements determine architecture.

Architecture determines design.

Design determines implementation.

And implementation determines requirements.

Be aware of these dependencies and be prepared to show the trace from requirements to architecture to design to implementation and back to requirements.

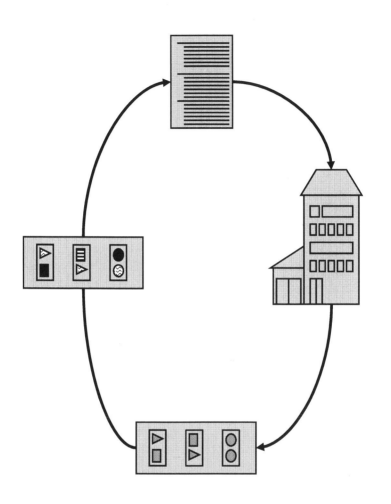

68.   DIVERGENCE

If requirements are unclear, incomplete or wrong then architecture will be unclear, incomplete or wrong.

And estimates will be unclear, incomplete or wrong. And design will be unclear, incomplete or wrong. And implementation will be unclear, incomplete or wrong.

Worse than that –divergence will ensure that the problems grow as you move away from requirements and towards implementation.

Watch out for divergence – make sure everything is as clear, complete and correct as possible.

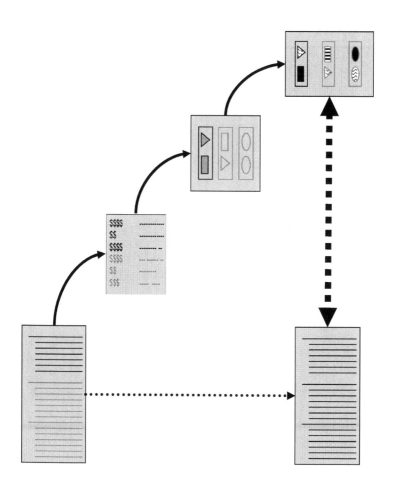

69.   THE COST OF OMISSION

What isn't discussed and covered in the architecture and design will emerge later as a problem or issue.

The cost to fix problems and issues caused by omissions at the architecture and design stages increases enormously as the process proceeds.

Get it right early in the planning and design. And make sure it is right at each stage in the process.

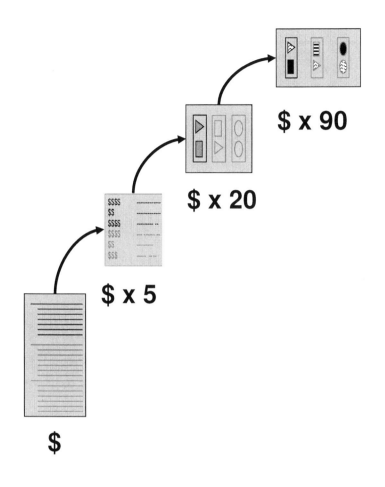

$ x 90

$ x 20

$ x 5

$

70.   COMMON SENSE AND THE OBVIOUS

Common sense isn't common. It often only becomes apparent because it has been overlooked.

The obvious isn't. People usually say "that's obvious" after the event – at a time when the obvious has emerged. It is only obvious because it has been articulated.

Discover sense – then make it commonly known. Tell people. Make it a basis for your architecture or designs.

Explain everything – even the obvious.

71.   SIMPLIFICATION

Simple is easier, and usually better, than complicated.

Simplify to understand, but don't over-simplify. As Einstein said, "Things should be as simple as possible, but no simpler."

Generalize to discover patterns, templates, principles and rules. But don't over-generalize.

Over-simplification, and over-generalization, often means that things get overlooked or forgotten.

And as Tom Gilb has said, "You may forget some critical factors, but they won't forget you."

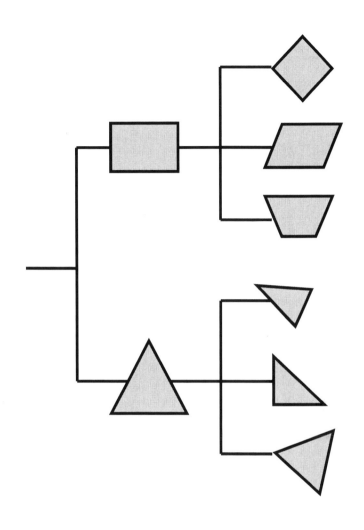

72.   REFLECTION

The more complex something is, the more you need to learn as you go and grow.

Allow time for reflection and learning.

Put it in the plan. Budget for it. Learn each step on the way.

When you discover problems and opportunities – adapt to them as early as possible and learn from these mistakes.

And check to see what the impact from your learning is.

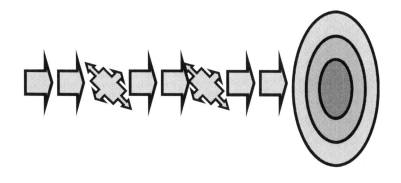

73. STRETCH VERSUS STRETCHED

We frequently find ourselves in situations that stretch our experience or skills. Too much stretch and we can end up out of our depth or beyond our comfort zone.

Stretching is a good way to challenge and extend your abilities,

Recognize the symptoms – take time out to ask someone, take a training course, or figure out what you are doing.

And remember Tom Gilb's good advice - "If you don't know what you're doing, don't do it on a large scale."

74.   QUICK AND DIRTY

We are sometimes forced to do things quickly, resulting in a design that isn't "clean".

Quick and dirty is OK - to experiment, or try out an idea.

But on its own it's not a good basis or formula for success. It's also not smart for building or maintaining a reputation for producing a quality result.

And quick and dirty isn't usually a good foundation for building upon.

Recognize the limitations of quick and dirty, and be prepared to refine and improve.

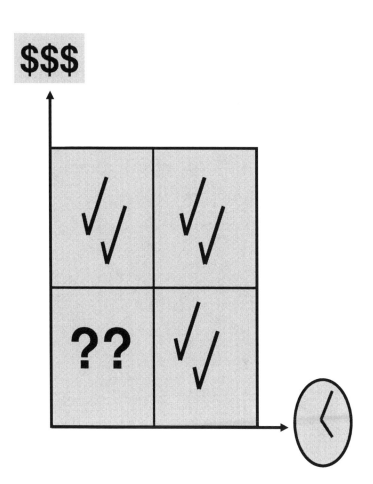

75.   TRUST

Integrity, trust and credibility make relationships, decisions, collaboration and progress easier.

A reputation for clear thinking and practical designs shows integrity, and helps to build trust and credibility.

Don't underestimate the part played by integrity, trust, and credibility.

76.   PRACTICALITY

Ideas are plentiful and easy to come by. We can all dream. We can all have a vision.

Making an idea work is more difficult and more important than having the idea.

Making ideas, concepts and dreams tangible, bringing them to life or fruition, takes time, persistence, ingenuity, skill and experience.

If you have an idea that is truly worthwhile, spend the time and effort to make it work, to bring it alive and introduce it into the practical world.

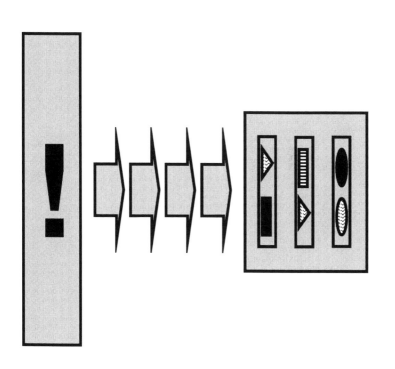

77.   PLAY WITH WORDS

How we communicate is coloured by the words we use. Some words are aggressive, others friendly; some encourage participation, or dissuade involvement. Some clarify, and some confuse and obfuscate.

Look at the words you use with a view to making each communication better.

Think about the difference between hand-off versus hand-shake; business alignment versus organizational fusion. And choose uplifting and heartening words.

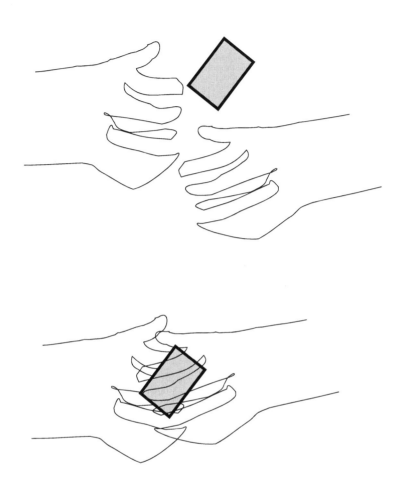

78.   MESSY OR NEAT

If you try something different, innovative, or original, then there are no precedents to follow.

If you conform to established standards and patterns, it's easier to build on a tried and tested foundation, allowing extra effort to go into creating a more finished and neat deliverable.

If your ideas or designs are not fully formed, you might find that they look rather fuzzy. This is natural – at first – but by the end, try to combine creativity with a smart and polished result.

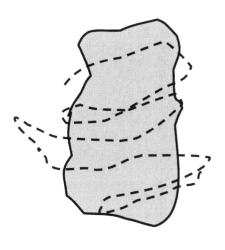

79. START AND ENDS

You can plan a journey from its start point, or plan your route by working back from the destination.

Similarly, with design you can analyze the current situation and decide what you would like to improve; or you can imagine what your ideal solution would be and figure out how to get there.

Identify the single start point – grounded in the real world and how things are today, and the many end points to what the future might provide.

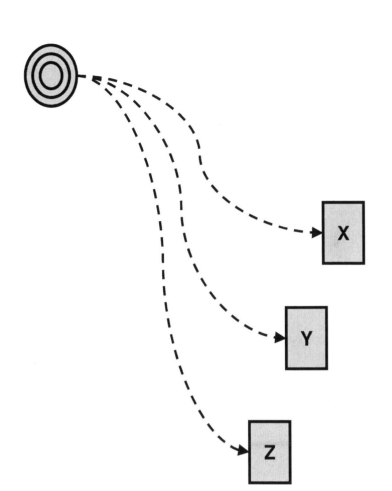

80.   A OR B?

Which comes first – the starting point or the end point?

Where you are or where you want to be?

Like the chicken and egg, when you are planning your journey from A to B both are equally important.

Know your current situation – it explains the limitations and issues you need to deal with.

Know your future state – it gives you direction, options and alternatives.

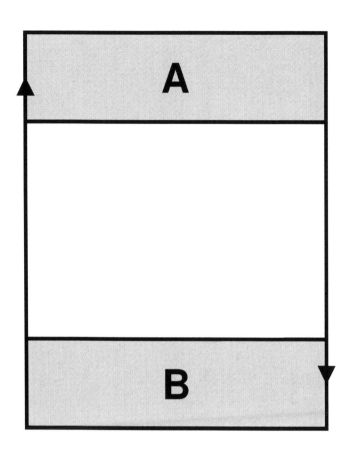

81.   ISSUES OR VISION

Too much emphasis analyzing your current situation can mean that you don't go anywhere. You get bogged down with the problems and issues – which can seem insurmountable: you can't hear the rhythm for the beating of the drums.

Too much emphasis visioning the future can create expectations that are difficult or impossible to realize. You can imagine the rhythm but you're not hearing the drums.

Aim for the right balance between the past, the present, and the future.

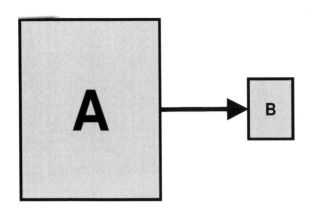

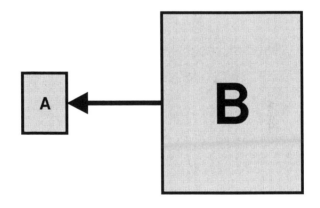

82.   6 UP, 9 DOWN

This isn't a crossword clue. 6 up, 9 down is a rule that carpenters follow to position hinges on a door.

The lower hinge is six inches up from the bottom of the door, and the upper hinge is nine inches down from the top of the door. The hinges appear to be equally proportioned.

Appearances and perceptions matter. Remember that how people see things is often more important than how they really are.

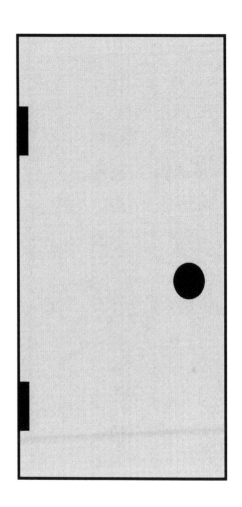

83. BROAD OR DEEP

Overviews need to be quick and broad without too much depth.

Detail needs take a bit longer, and need to be deep and not too broad.

The full picture results from a single broad overview, supported by a number of deep detailed views.

Look at all the options – quickly, and at a high-level.

Then explore your selection – quickly, but in detail.

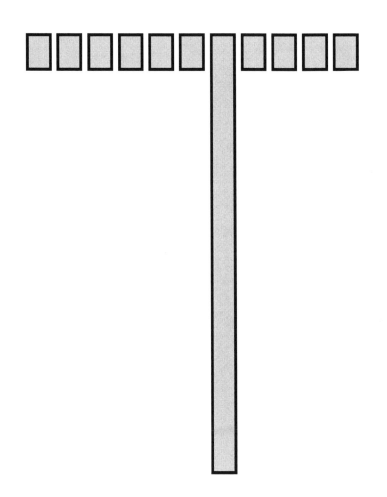

84. WORK THE WHITE SPACE

White spaces are the gaps between.

Sometimes gaps need to be filled.

Sometimes white space needs to be added – the silence between beats.

Look for the white space in your designs and solutions.

Sometimes you need to reduce the intensity of your design – adding breathing space.

Sometimes you will need to close a gap and fill some of the space.

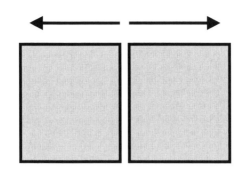

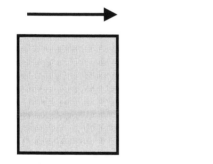

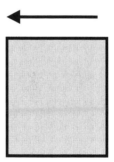

85.   THE JOURNEY AND THE DESTINATION

Some say the journey is more important than the destination.

Some say the destination has greater significance.

As you analyze, architect, design and develop, new ideas and alternatives will appear.

So – which is more important – sticking rigidly to your original destination or target, or taking new ideas on board?

Keep the destination in mind, but enjoy the journey. If you're on a journey, know how to spot a destination when you get there.

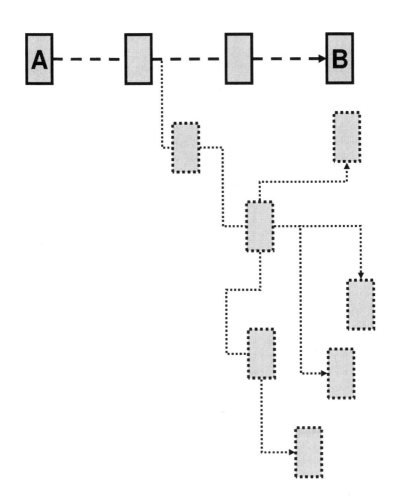

86.   DEGREE AND PACE OF CHANGE

A newspaper, a stock list, a catalogue and a novel.

A newspaper has totally different content every day. Items on a stock list change at different rates depending on demand and supply. A catalogue has a new edition every season. A novel might go through several drafts, but remain unchanged following publication.

Each has a different degree of change and a different pace of change.

Only change requirements and designs and keep them up-to-date when there is a good reason for doing so.

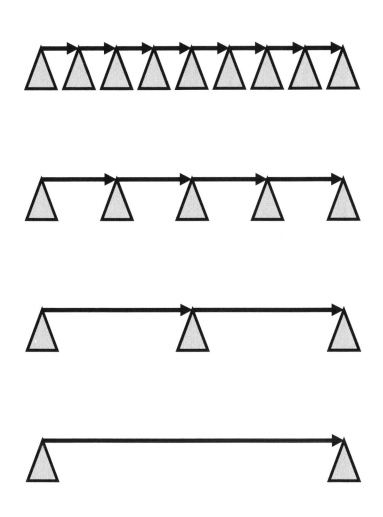

87.   THE KEY TO A CLOSED DOOR

Diagrams can be hard or impossible to interpret without a key to explain what is meant by differences in shape or colour.

What is the difference between a square and a circle? Why some shapes are coloured green while others are blue? What do the arrows mean? Why are some lines dashed and others not?

If you draw diagrams to show your ideas and designs, include the key to unlock otherwise hidden meaning.

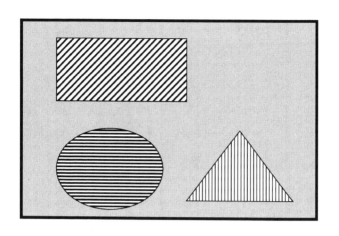

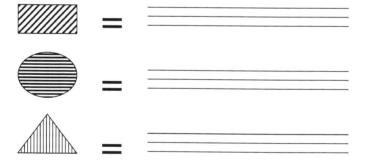

88. DIFFERENCE AND SIMILARITY

There are many types of diagram, but sometimes an apparently dissimilar diagram is simply a different way of representing the same thing.

Take a hub-and-spoke, node-and-link, or hierarchy.

Each looks fundamentally different – but the same content can be shown to different effect with each diagram style.

Choose a diagram or representation that best conveys your ideas or design.

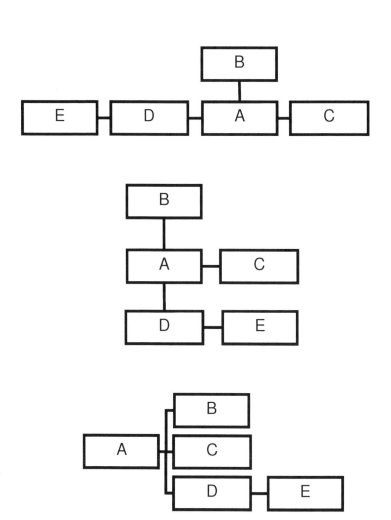

89. AGENDAS AND MINUTES

Meetings are a major source of requirements and design decisions. But this information is not always captured.

When there is useful discussion at a meeting it is always worth recording.

Send the documented minutes to attendees and get them validated.

If there are any disagreements, corrections or changes, add them to the document.

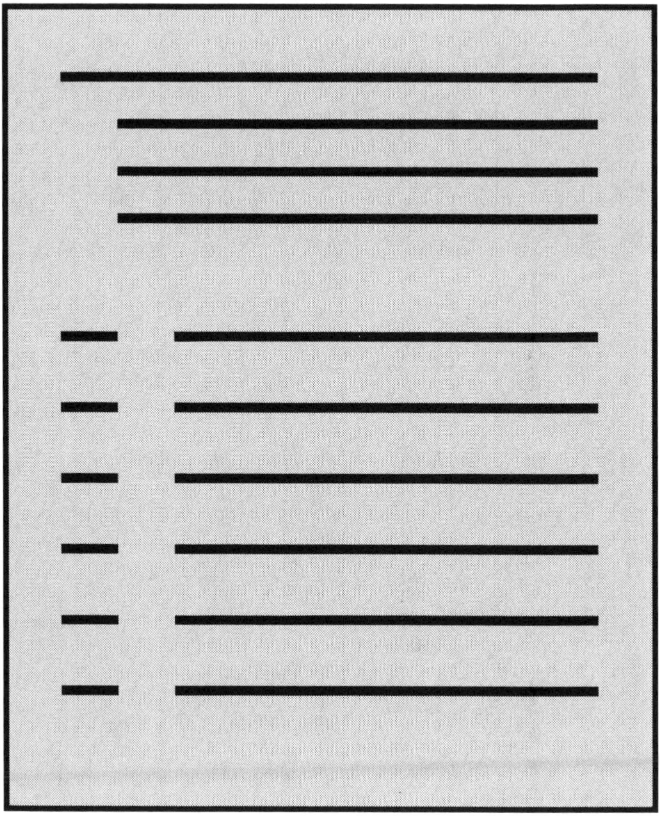

90. SUFFICIENT SOPHISTICATION

For a novice it's not easy to play the piano or guitar. Effort, time and discipline are needed to develop skills and capability. Then it becomes easier.

It is impossible to make a musical instrument intrinsically easier to play by simplifying or changing its design. This would destroy the sufficient sophistication that the piano, guitar, or design needs.

Don't sacrifice sufficient sophistication for the sake of ease of use. Ease of use is a great design principle; but sometimes it should only be easy to use with knowledge and experience.

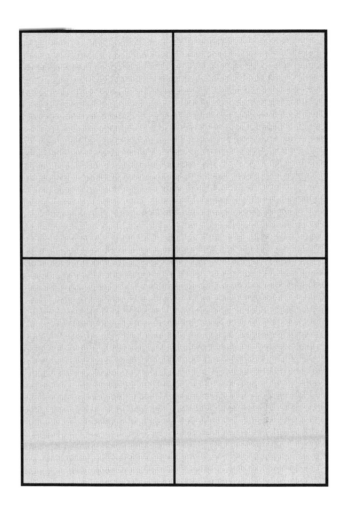

91.   BALANCE

People will be deterred from using your design if it takes a lot of effort to understand and learn how to use it.

People will be prepared to spend the time and effort learning how to use your design, or learning about more sophisticated features, if it is of use to them.

Create a balance between the efforts or time (to the user) required to learn to use your design against the perceived value or benefit from using the design.

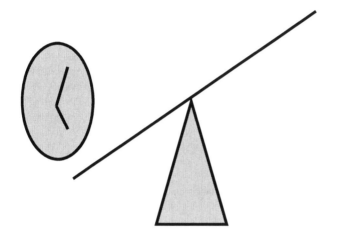

92. DESIGN AND USE

There is an iterative cycle – of design and use.

Design creates new possibilities.

Use reveals new ways of using the design, problems with the design, and new requirements.

This allows design to create new possibilities.

Which allows us to reveal…

Observe how people use your architecture or designs, and use this is input to your future designs.

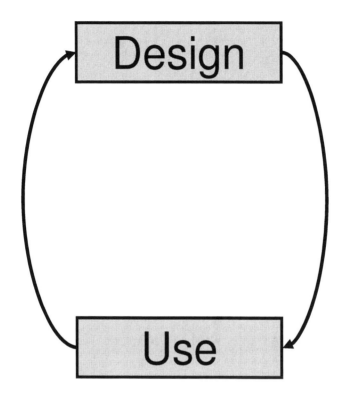

93.   ENDURANCE

In the long run, as Joseph Bradsky has observed, "Ruins are the most persistent form of architecture."

Everything has its time. Some things last longer than others.

But while physical things fall into disrepair and decline, ideas can continue to influence for many generations.

To achieve immortality create persistent and enduring ideas and designs that influence a wider range of people. These are ideas that evolve or get incorporated into new ideas.

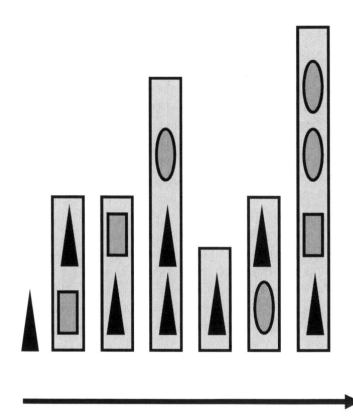

94.   DESIGN = FORM + CONTENT

In 1964, Marshall McLuhan famously stated that "the medium is the message".

How a design conveys a message – the form – becomes an important part of the message.

What the message conveys – the content – determines how the message is conveyed.

Form can change the message in the content.

Think about form and content together – as a horse and carriage, or love and marriage.

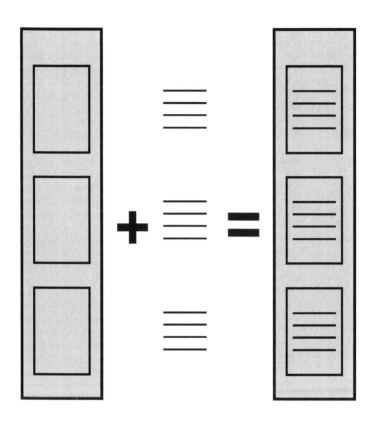

95. TEMPLATES AND PRINCIPLES

Templates and principles - to paraphrase Einstein talking of Le Corbusier's proportional system - make the good better and the bad difficult.

Use pre-defined templates and principles to improve a design and to avoid design mistakes.

But design can't be adduced from templates and principles alone. They need the addition of content.

Adapt templates and principles when necessary to suit need.

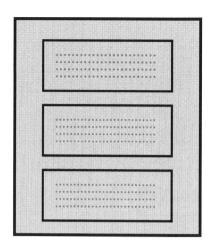

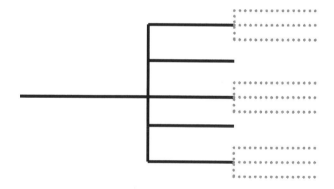

96. BLACK BOX

Black box design is a great idea – hide the detailed design inside a black box, and the box can be used without needing to know its interior workings.

But even a black box has to be documented somewhere. It is dangerous to have a black box where the design is impossible to get at. Someone needs the skill to understand the inside of the black box.

When you use a design aid like a black box, you need to know enough about how it works to be able to use it effectively.

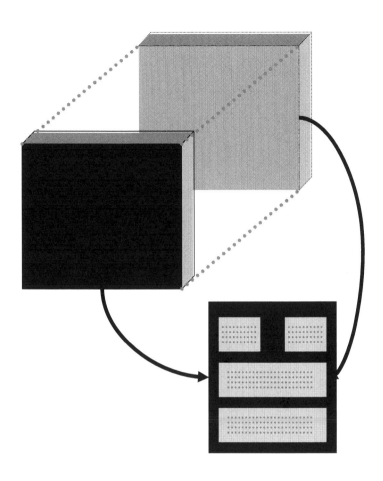

97.   FAMILIES INHERIT DNA

Some components designs belong to a family of similar things. They inherit components, relationships, patterns, rules and ideas from parent designs. And in turn those parent designs inherit from their parents.

Define a common ancestor design to make it easier to specify generic components that then cascade down to family members further down the descendant hierarchy.

Each generation can accept the inherited components, or accept exceptions that explain how, and why, the inheritance is changed.

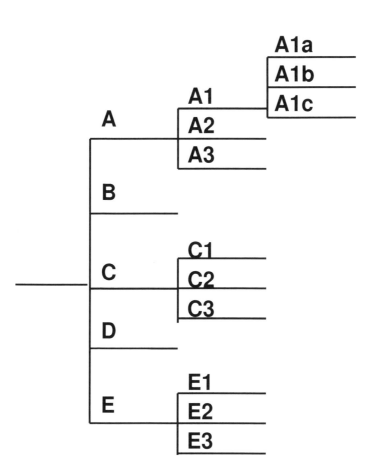

98.   LANGUAGE

We use language to explain our needs and requirements. But language is open to interpretation and misunderstanding.

Define any word or phrase that is likely to cause confusion.

These definitions explicitly document the language used by members of a community.

This community often relates to, or is based around, a domain of knowledge – or subject domain. The definitions form part of the language of a domain.

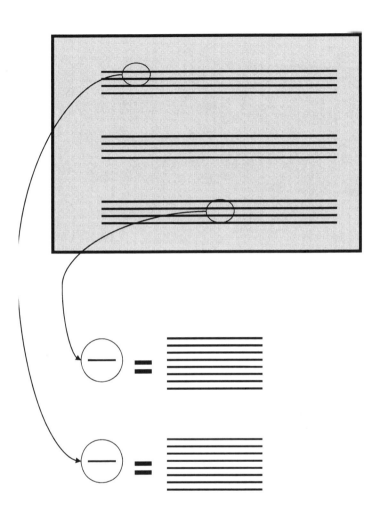

99.   DESIGN LANGUAGE

The language of a domain can be extended beyond words and phrases to form a comprehensive language for design.

Like any language, a design language brings consistency and coherence, quality and structure.

Help to create the design language for your domain. It can include such things as frameworks, templates, patterns, principles, and checklists.

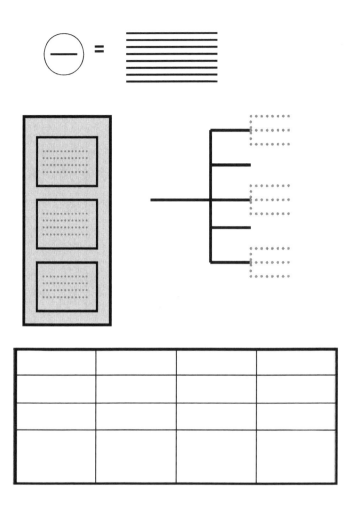

100. CONSISTENCY AND RIGIDITY

A design language is a very powerful design tool – it simplifies the design process by providing components that can be tailored to form a significant part of a final design.

But a design language can become so well established that it is regarded as fixed and unchangeable. Changes to a dominant design language can take many years.

If you challenge established styles, demonstrate that your ideas are a better, cheaper, or quicker alternative – and gain a following of influential users.

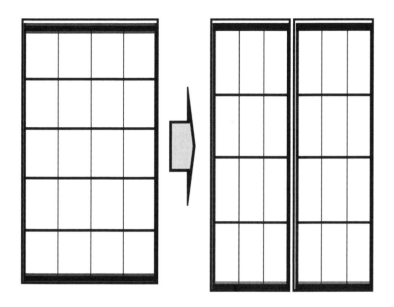

101. CHECK EVERYTHING PERSONALLY

You know what you know; you don't know what others know. Can you trust what they tell you?

You know your weaknesses. You need to get to know the weaknesses (and strengths) of others.

Work like a historian - keep a note of all sources; distinguish between primary (first hand) sources, and secondary (beware of Chinese whispers).

There are 101 tips and guidelines in this book. Are there 101 tips and guidelines in this book?

101

For further books, courses, and other materials related to Enterprise Architecture, please visit my web site: www.evernden.net

40762957R00124

Made in the USA
Charleston, SC
13 April 2015